An attempt at comfort

Someday, someone might dive into a pool of emotions where the tide will rip them into an undertow of unending stupidity, obsession, anxiety and loneliness. It's a tale told too many times. I hope my words might be a kind of rescue boat, a buoy, to pull them warm metal graced by the shade of a nearby tree. Just breathe the air of our little blue sphere and calm, you'll be okay.

Chapter 1: Spring
.... 04

Chapter 2: Summer
.... 18

Chapter 3: Autumn
.... 33

Chapter 4: Winter

.... 49

Chapter 1

I was once told that I was born with my umbilical cord wrapped around my neck. I can only imagine from my current hardships, I must have persevered the same emotions then as I am now. Hung in my past life, for my skin color? For being my most authentic self? or I must have been the most infamous cowboy in the wild wild west! In the spring we sprout seeds to sprout each flower with its blooming petals. I was born but I don't know if I was ever growing, not the way I think I needed, or even wanted to.

Spring

I open my petals,
Because I hope to be bright and beautiful,
Even if my colors are purple and black.
I sharpen my thorns
To keep myself from being eaten up
By the wild beasts of the forest.

The sun and moon shine far.
The river runs fast and wild.
Every splash of water, a new leaf on my stem,
The sun's light is harsh
The warmth is too much.
The moon makes up for the sun
When he isn't around
She's too scared to cool down.

The light from the sky
Hidden by the width of other flowers.
Thank god for the river.

Helium

I become a balloon
Filled with nothing but your lies
Floating so far high

From now on I've decided
That once I pop
Maybe I'll come down.

The tenacity of my shell
Keeps your helium from leaking
And letting me down

And once I reach the sun
I'll finally find what I'm looking for,
The warmth that your cold heart
Has been giving me
Breath by breath.

Push/Pull

When the sun fades into the floor

And the moon rises to take watch

I leave the front light on

So that when the knocking comes

I know if it's the song of bird

Or the whistle of the wind

When the wolf comes to huff puff

And blow it all down.

Snail

5am,
Or the middle of the day
Someone is dying,
And someday,
That person will be me.

I fear that place
The void of darkness,
And it's picked white fences,
So barren and cold.

The end of the cosmos
Or a speeding car.
I just wish to be immortal

So I'm never lonely,
I'm 17...

I don't want to die

Desires

Declare your love my own,

Even when it's not.

Simply so that

I may break my own heart.

Realize that to blindly

Envision love

It's nothing more...

It's simply a desire.

Viper

Venom is the fear that flows

Inside the veins of

Prey that don't check

Every corner and

Refuse to be patient

Celestial bodies

To live on one sphere

Yet on two different worlds,

Our realms remain breached.

For you page

It's never for me
When I'm bored
I pain my thumbs
To feel something
And every time
It's always praise for the
Tall muscular white men
With their curly straight hair

2.8
For simply existing
With their smile

That stupid ass smile

I'm not surprised that
I expect to be alone

"fyp" "for you page"
Or the "haha they won't like you, feels bad page

Invincible

It always seemed to me that

To each their own tale

Would mean that to each person

They're the main character

Whom is bound to the culmination

And would watch everything fall

Just before the cracks

Would take their shadow.

The gay agenda

Wake up

"Morning routine"

Check phone, Email and funds

Breakfast

Pickup coffee

School work (optional)

9-5 work

Gas car on the way home

Dinner

Take over the world

Sleep

Repeat

Caterpillar of love

It's the kind of butterflies that leave me stuck

I begin to rest in my cocoon

In the hopes I can fly away

Far- far away from the chirps of you and your chicks.

Derek

Trap me..

For I was too foolish..

To turn into safety.

I'd stick my foot

In the rope

Hoping I could nourish your needs.

So when you find me

Please be grateful

That you caught something

In the first place.

The closet

The door has rails,

and that day, so was I.

All my outfits...

it took me so long to leave

and they still look like shit.

I hide here

from judgment and pain

the hanging belt

will scar past my skin.

The mirror outside

don't recognize me.

I came out?

He continues to invite me back in.

The closet is unforgiving.

3.13.20

It's gonna be a fruitless July

For these seeds don't usually sprout in spring

And with the tension of the heat

Nothings coming out of the ground during June

For the past three years nothing has grown

Lumberjacks had come by

Stripping the forest of the few trees

Then set up a fence

Keeping the forest from growing out

The vines just want fresh water.

Summer

In the day, I'm forced to open up
And show my petals
Behind the thorns, My petals still burn
My roots hide beneath the ground
To keep from drying up
And falling out of place

During the night
I must close my wingspan of colors
Even when I try to enjoy the sun's absence
The moon doesn't like it
She's worried that the river stained me
She tries to come closer to the earth
To keep the river from drowning me out,
The river was already drying up anyway.

I miss the river
Not every droplet was kind,
But it was always refreshing.
—--------

Chapter 2

I'd like to think every child looks forward to their summer, the sweets of the melting ice cream, the long rides to amusement parks and the fair, to restaurants that you wouldn't normally be able to go to because tonight's a school night, to spend the saved-up money on some sunglasses or a videogame that you can't play unless its 100 degrees out or time at a friend's house. I hold on to those hopes because while I might miss the teachers that kept me busy, I'd love to think that as a 19-year-old I'm living the life romanticized for us by each of the four seasons of Sixteen. Even if I'm sad and anxious when I lie in my bed.

Blood

Does it warm you,
My attention your stealing,
Does it ever come to mind you should bother me,
So self-consciously,
Does it ever crawl in your skin and give you a feeling,
A feeling of sinking?
A feeling you were never a problem?
There were two ways to solve this mystery,
By accepting or leaving,
Stay sober or drink it.

Break my heart or seek it.
Love me & don't abuse it.
Our love, Let's keep it.
Overdose on it.
Demand it...

It's in my blood,
I feel it.
I love him...
—--------

KissURN

Never have I been so thirsty

For the drink of person

Until I laid eyes on you

And hopefully my lips,

Might be blessed with a taste

Of your lips.

———-------

18

I'm too young to be an adult,
Too old to be a child...

Too uninvolved with my family,
Cause I don't get along with anyone of them.
Always wanna tell me how to feel and how I feel,
But wonders why I don't open up...
Wanna know what I need them to do
For me to be comfortable,
Never changes, instead, expects me to change.
"The real world isn't fair",
But throw tantrums when they don't get what they
want...

Romanticize my teenage years,
And expect me to be happy I got down played
For shit like this..

Feels great to be 18!
—--------

Pluto

I'm dancing around fire fuckin with y'all
And it's hard to be declared
When the solar system has no room
For babies like me
I'm a fragile ball of ice...
I get too close
And I burn
And if I'm not close enough
I'm dropped and shatter
into a million pieces

I love y'all but damn
It's hard being Pluto
—-------

Ferris wheel

You're a roller coaster,

In most cases

You're fast and rough.

This time I ask if you could be a Ferris wheel

Go slow,

Lift me up and down

And when I'm on top

I want to admire the stars.

—-------

I liked my bully in elementary school

He calls me bro, brosky and dude,
Just as if he doesn't know my name.
What do "bros" do?
Because boyfriends might know each other's taste,
But bros don't fuck, the way a married couple might.

Bros don't crave each other
The way he texts me,
When he's bored and lonely.

If I meet him in the park...
Will he hold my hand in public
Like how it was locked in his girlfriend's on the school
bus?
Will he hold my neck if we kiss
As if he was still bullying me, like in the 6th grade?
————------

RnB

The swing of his hips

Keep me locked in some kind of dance

And my legs quake for more.

My heart pumps to his rhythm.

My mind is in places

Only sopranos could reach.

—-------

A trip in Monterey

How might one describe love?

Could it be the weight of the water and sand

That leave bits and pieces of memory

Tangled in your hair?

When you wash it out

Will you watch it drain and remember me?

———-------

It's not a cloak, it's a blankly

Sleep helps kill the time

So when I might pass

Closing my eyes to rest

Won't feel unfamiliar...

It's a glimpse into death

I dream of the afterlife

God forbid I dream

Of an average day any longer

—-------

Sweaters in June

Sweaters in June

Keep my skin warm

When it misses the heat

His fingertips radiate

From my inside

Out.

—-------

Attached

It's the shit you say

The things that you do

Even when it's not about me

That attachment,

The before and after transactions.

—-------

Colors

Red, my face when you make me blush.
Blue, as you steal my breath
Purple, the magic of your soft words
Yellow, your rays of light inspire
Green, as my leaves grow
Orange, the warmth of your arms

Red, blood running off my beat face
Blue, as you rip the air from my lungs
Purple, when your knuckles love my skin
Yellow, the most hazards of your parts
Green, the envy of my simple life
Orange, your fire and rage

———-------

Eternals

Life comes to a climax-

So I wish they'd speak of us

As the unending,

The constant expanse of the cosmos

That might bring upon our love.

Roses always wither…

—-------

Summer nights

You reminisce on the days you wouldn't ever see it

Cause "These faggots trying to be Superman".

I wish for the day I wouldn't get hate or killed

For wanting to be Superman..

Summer nights are for comics, jokes, road trips and

hanging with your loved ones...

Not hanging with your loved ones...

———-------

Chapter 3

After such a short time the sunshine ends and the weather cools. Life begins and the unending happiness ends. At 19 I fear I'm to truly become an adult. I'm scared that I might not fall in love because every relationship has fallen apart. Every friendship feels like shaky ground and I often doubt the loyalties, my credit card consumes more than I can feed it and I only hope that one day I learn to tame that beast. I hope that one day I'll be happy with who I am and there might not be anything to stop the growth, but autumn has begun and the leaves on the shady tree crumple under the pressure of joyus feet.

Autumn

The clouds grow pink during the day,
The stars shine through during the night,
The river is filled with leaves,
Most of them are mine,
Malnourished and dry,
I cut them off and move on.

I know that new leaves will come,
Even if it takes longer than I hoped,
The river gets colder,
The sun and moon are colder,
The other flowers are harder to recognise
When the shadows are being so heavy on me
And yet I must push their petals up
Everytime their colors are lacking...

Soon my petals will wilt,
The cool breeze,
Warns for a harsh winter.

——-------

10.30.19

His blue blanket.
The one I'd never asked for,
But was thankful to have.

It kept me from the cold,
As thorns
Keeping it's leaves from the jaws
Of a much larger beast.

It would sprout an idea
to grow in my garden.
A blue rose,

Creased to entertain the sun,
But let the sun keep lit
Because as far as he believes,
Love is a two way street.

Thus when the petals wilt,
And the thorns dull,
It won't be unattainable,
Because the roses never grew.

—-------

Broken melodies

For when he breaks your heart

And if you come crying

For the aid of my shoulder.

Remember that it couldn't be me,

You never gave me that opportunity

—-------

Food poisoning

Like unseasoned chicken or a bland soup,
You bring nothing to the table,
And while the broth may look nice,
It's missing a certain thickness
That your bitterness makes up for.

Change the lighting,
Add some cilantro and you might not notice
The rest of the ingredients are spoiled

With one inconvenience you push for
Oppression appeal,
Why cry when a customer returns the dish with a
complaint
Bitch just add the fucking pepper
Otherwise, refund them and move on
If it was spicy when it needed to be
We wouldn't have a problem.

Now you don't want color on your meat,
But you want all the textures
An ethnic and cultured soup comes with...

Humble yourself
Next time you turn in the mirror
To convince yourself
Something is back there.
—--------

Notify me

I'm tired of looking

For a feeling from my screen

The buzzing that signals

That you thought of me.

—--------

Second-hand smoke

Imagine, you're so in love,
They move you so much,
Lights a fire in you that you once believed
Was blown out for good.

Its for the better
You're better
Kind of like a breath of fresh air
They help you move from your problems
All they have to do is smile
It clears your mind
Only to drench it in their scent.

Mid-thought, the door will open and guess who
Its them
Everytime its them

That cigarette keeps you company in conversation
Because while they keep you hooked on their warmth
You're suffocating from the smoke
It kills you on the inside,
Feeding on something you shouldn't have
And the longer you hold on
The more it melts
The more it will burn when you put it out.

—------

Self respect is something only you can earn,

And it took me so long to lose it,

The will to change.

——------

Udon-needed me again

Like Chopsticks

We only come together

When we need something.

———------

Sad boy Insta subs

I'm too busy crying over you
To think about you.
The emotional toll it takes,
The physical effort...
It's too great to pain my thumbs
With the knowledge of you.

He's got a new man,
A new car,
Even a tattoo.
He's happy...

I just can't help but be jealous
Because I could be doing better,
And I will...
But it's easier to cry
Cause we could have had that, together.
—-------

He's a bitch

He's a bitch
Exists Apart from
Several words but as

An Anagram for when he

Brings around the negative and
Induces a sense of anxiousness,
Trauma and drama
Circulating around
Himself and into your life...
—------

Love sick songs

I dance with the memory of you
Because you were the only one
Who didn't put a bullet in my foot
To keep me from moving
So that they could keep spinning
Circles around my mind
And haunt me with the memory

That they left.

The melody is good

But you're not the one...

Skip

———-------

Your word

In my reality

The only truth there,

Was That you weren't,

Because you're too honest,

For that kind of hope.

——-------

Chip Skylark

Now you're gone, I can finally smile.

The cavity in my mouth

keeps me from speaking when they're in front,

I became conscious of my smile

I seal my words in

And my head lets out only negative thoughts

And regret,

It was embarrassing to bring you up

I don't want you… no one does

So now that you're gone, I can finally smile

My shiny teeth and me

—--------

Light switch

Conditional oppression

Is a term I like to use when white twinks
Feel like they aren't getting enough attention for
existing
So being gay becomes their biggest problem
Conditional oppression
Benefits off of moments when
Old white people
can't purchase
Their favorite brand of make up
At a small business
When they can't cover their racist comments
Behind the mask keeping others safe
Conditional oppression
Represents moments when
Straight men are jealous
Because two men
get a fifteen second scene of intimacy
Conditional oppression
Prospers
When gym bros
Rage because
someone tries to diet
Or is comfortable and loves
Their own body
Oppression isn't a light switch you can just flip...
The condition of not liking what you see,
The fact that you can't have "it"
And when you have to be considerate
Aren't reasons that could get you killed

Frozen heart

The touch of your skin

Leaves the cold chills of ice

Frozen by your heart

—-------

Chapter 4

I fear for the day I grow old, I wish I might not ever see the light. I wish I couldn't give false hopes of lots of treasure on my deathbed. I don't want a deathbed. I want to live forever, but with the friendships I have, I hold on to the thought that my relationships aren't like the famous rose poems, and their flourishing petals brighten the love between two persons. Roses die, like any other living thing. With all this worrying I come to realize I'm only 19. While it feels like I wasn't born yesterday, I've got a long ways before I am even close to cashing out on my social security tax.

Winter

What hasn't fallen off my stem
Freezes.
From the sky falls salty white snow,
It becomes cold and unbearable.
The sun and moon are gone
Hidden by colossal gray clouds.

The river has frozen
The moisture of the snow
Is not enough to sustain,
I don't have seeds to drop dormant.
With no water I have no energy to stay open.
The petals close, the sky falls forever
Soon it might stop.
All I can do is wait.

Buried under sleet and snow
I can no longer climb up for warmth
I die.
——-----

December

I wanted to kiss you, so you might be so shocked,

That you would've stopped and appreciated how much I

liked you,

When she couldn't bother knowing your name.

But you ghosted a sinner, past tense.

—-------

Blue diamonds

Your hand slides down the side of my face
So softly you caress my skin,
Rough and saddened over time,

When I cry you look in my eyes

Like your world has been shattered.

Grab me tight and hold me close,

The words you speak

"I love you"

Suffocate my air

Keeping me silent

My shoulders stained

With the dark tint

Of your runny crystal rain drops.

————-------

Stitches

Tearing the tears off my heart

So you might not see it

But all I seem to remove

Are the clots of blood

And the stitches

Keeping me sewn up.

—--------

Hope for you

The uncertainty

Of you coming back

When I let go

Is why I haven't yet.

But I'm scared,

Even with the reasons

That you should have been gone

I might still stay.

—--------

Fire drill

We can't burn away our problems
Because fire can't kill fire,

I begin to turn the wheel
And everything is warm
At last I've found it
The heat becomes comforting,

It drowns the problems
Faster than any Liquor.

To cope in this space
Becomes an act of arson,
I destroy the home
That I never owned
And reason with the demons
That you tell me
Were never there.

I begin to wonder,
How'd you come about?

"9-1-1
What's your emergency?"
"A home is on fire
And someone is inside.."
—-------

So you've decided to quit being the moon

My craters are deep

I'm tired of astral dust

Brushing my surface,

With no core to erupt and fill them...

I'm tired of taking care

Of this world when it mocks me

When it has its own problems

That suffocate and burn it.

I wish I could move away somewhere

With a orbit of my own,

I would have many rings and wouldn't need moons,

I'd have warmth inside and water to keep me cool.

I don't want to be the moon of his any longer...

——-----

Ego

The way you rose up,

And began to shout

Till everyone noticed you shine,

Was the same way that I

Grew silent.

I followed you and still

You only saw me for my faults.

—-------

Doctors note

To whom it may concern,
This patient is currently under medical care.

Thus is under no circumstances
Allowed to return to your direct environment.

Activity is restricted as follows:
Stressful situations,
Over complications,
And lastly,
Any application of heartbreak,

Sincerely,
—-------

Screw you

Screw you,

Could you stop

Receiving nothing

Except unconditional

Welcoming and love?

You're perfect,

Observe is all I ask

Understand me.

—-----

"Submissive"

I'm a submissive bitch,

I've got too little emotion to spend

Too little fucks to give,

I'll just bruise and be disappointed

The next time you hurt me.

—------

Charon's obol

You wanna be cremated when you die,

I'm not sure how I wanna die,

But I hope

It won't be forceful cremation

Buried 20ft under

Or lost at sea when the ice caps melt

Flooding the world

Your gold Jar will keep you safe in

You've got the coin to afford it.

—------

Canciones reconfortantes

It was cute when he sent me songs,

I just wish I would have listened.

The next time my phone pings I hope its,

"I wish I could give you what you want

but we both know I can't." again

The way you broke my heart,

Felt comfortable.

"Buenos noches."

"Yeah, you too"

—-------

Dyslexic dreams

To: _ _ _ _ _

I dreamt of you last night

And the night before,

Nothing weird really

You just apologized

And I'm not really sure for what

—--------

Platonic

Sometimes I can't trust

My friends with my things

I become anxious to hear

Them read the poems

I wrote about them

—-------

I HATE YOU

I wish I never met you

Having to forget you

And to forget why,

Thinking you could change

Every time I come back.

You were the colonist,

Overtook and conquered

Unconsolidated mind spaces.

—-------

"1955"

I cried on the bus

cause when I wanted to be one of the cool kids.

I was asked to sit in the front seat

where the bus driver could keep an eye on me

and y'all could act an ass

I cried because I didn't understand

Why couldn't she trust me?

———------

Unusual cliché

If you're out there

Please tell me where you are

Because I'm desperate for the touch of one

And I'd hate to use the cliché

"Where were you all this time"

It feels like right now I need you

More than ever

————-------

Sucker for pain

My heart breaks over you

And like a masochist

I heal just so I might be able to do it all over again

—-------

DTR

It's a slow knife
and I can't find the hand
pushing it deeper
cause' my eyes are locked into yours
When you're not even looking here...

The sharp pain of the knife's twist
and the edges leak blood
I feel like there's a hole in my chest
Good friends wouldn't break each other's hearts, right?

I pull out the knife with the same hands that inserted
such a blade-
and begin to stitch myself up
So when the next guy comes around
My gay little heart might see the scar
Before my eyes do.
—-------

"Being so deprived of a loving relationship has fucked with the

boundaries I have with straight men or even men that I shouldn't

be romantically invested in and I fall so easily because I haven't

been treated correctly or even shown direct attention from anyone,

that play flirting and doing things that apply to my wants and needs

become deathly Infatuating and overwhelming."

If God is somewhere out there

So let your God be real

I demand an apology from her...

These blessings could never equate

To the pain and grief I've lived through.

The anxious and darkened moments,

In fear that she doesn't love me.

—-------

"Happier than ever"

Ask yourself:

Who would have endlessly tried to get another man

pregnant

What kind of flowers are in our vases

When it goes wrong for you & her I'll have a husband of

my own

Where all of our Polaroids are snapped

Why you didn't choose me- won't come across your

mind,

How you dodged happier than ever will be

and I won't feel bad at all.

Heartbreak is a meth lab for my poems

While it's fattening to eat these emotions

Writing these poems serves as an exercise for my hands

 and thumbs to paint onto paper and pen.

So I don't think tonight I will stop listening to moody

Spotify songs

and endlessly typing the same emotions till it's weird-

 I'll fall asleep before I consciously halt